Body to Brain

— STEW ROSS —

— Illustrated by Stu Sedgwick —

An environmentally friendly book printed and bound in England by
www.printondemand-worldwide.com

 Mixed Sources
Product group from well-managed forests, and other controlled sources
www.fsc.org Cert no. TT-COC-002641
© 1996 Forest Stewardship Council

 PEFC Certified
This product is from sustainably managed forests and controlled sources
www.pefc.org
PEFC/16-33-415

This book is made entirely of chain-of-custody materials

Stew Ross

www.fast-print.net/store.php

Body to Brain
Copyright © Stew Ross & Stu Sedgwick 2012

All rights reserved

No part of this book may be reproduced in any form by photocopying or any electronic or mechanical means, including information storage or retrieval systems, without permission in writing from both the copyright owner and the publisher of the book.

ISBN 978-178035-503-0

First published 2012 by
FASTPRINT PUBLISHING
Peterborough, England.

Body to Brain

Stew Ross

Stewart Ross, singer, songwriter, poet ,mandolin player and guitarist has roots set deep in his celtic origins, living and working on the south coast in Littlehampton ,he continues to write and develop his individual mix of songs and powerful poetry, promoting original music and the spoken word,

Stu Sedgwick

Stu Sedgwick has been an engineer for the last 25 years in fields as diverse as Aeronautics, Cryogenics and Horticulture. He currently resides in West Sussex where he is an Engineering Manager. Cynic, Realist, Scientist, Cartoonist, always questioning "why?" This book was therefore, the perfect vehicle to portray the slightly stranger side of everyday life.

Body to Brain

WHY?

Relentless rambling!
Diffused clarity!
Induced opacity!
Confusion reigns!

Impose your will little autocrat,
We no longer hear nor do your bidding!

It's easy to destroy, to demoralise, to disempower,
To ask the question why? And why?..... And why?

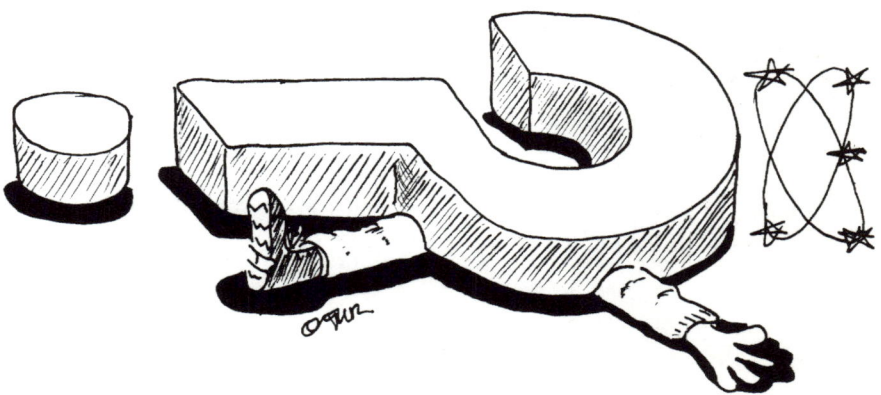

Stew Ross

PANTS

Overheard a conversation about comfortable pants,
Tween two of my favourite, matriarchal aunts,
The type of pants from M&S, really big in size,
That keep your bits and pieces warm,
That should please lustful eyes.

The type which prove essential, on having hips replaced,
They hold you all together, where prosthetics have been placed,
They cover up embarrassment, the instructions will divulge,
By deftly placing pressure, all around your irksome bulge.

"My bones are getting harder" said one aunt to the other,
Whilst her auntly audience, seemed more concerned with blubber,
Measuring her belly against the freezer door,
And thinking to herself, "these pants aint working any more!"

"I'm sorry dear?"... "Did I hear you right?"
"You once phoned Douglas Bader?"
"Oh bother! Would you look at that! I've got another ladder!"
"I'll have to wait till Thursday week, till I get my pension money"
"To be without supporting tights– now –simply isn't funny!"

"Come dear! Concentrate! I spoke about my bones!"
"I do wish you would listen to the nature of my moans"
"I believe you're turning deaf and undeniably round"
"Turning down the waistband dear, gives best control I've found."

"These pants are oh so comfy! And give great satisfaction"
"And as a Brucey bonus, they've reduced my gut a fraction"
"And as for you dear, I imagine you're just the same"
"You hide your key beneath the flap within the con-trol pane"
"The elasticated panel which your belly will resist,"
"The freedom that your YULDI (1) knew will now be sorely missed!"

- 4 -

Body to Brain

The benefits of comfy pants, let no man cast asunder!
They're built to last, contain a blast,
And control your thighs of thunder.
They're trimmed with fancy lacy beads,
In colours green to russet,
The designers sympathetic cut brings airflow to the gusset.

A most important attribute, one that your mother knew,
Essential wind, around, behind, keeps all things fresh it's true,
And when they're new, just out the bag,
There's nothing so fantastic, than strolling out with confidence,
Trussed up in new elastic.

The ideal shape our aunts pursue with escalating vigour,
Inspired some famous corsetiere to define the perfect figure,
Figures such as hour glass, elongated pear,
Calculated distance, from here to over there,

Material selection, ergonomics…….. risk,
Strategic pocket placement, in which to store the whisk,
Observating zipper speed at which to disencumber,
Panic stricken emergers from unexpected slumber,

Stew Ross

Parameters for garb design in bodily restriction,
Consideration given, to coefficients of friction,
Wind speed and direction, incidents of chaff,
Likely outcomes, consequence of over zealous laugh,

The elements of great design combine to spawn a winner,
The answer to most women's prayers,
A pant to make you thinner !!!!!!!!!!!

GOD BLESS M&S

Body to Brain

(1) YULDI...God walks down the line of babies doing his pre despatch quality check, points at the relevant babies' belly button and declares "YULDI" (you'll do), hence it came to pass that your belly button is known as a YULDI.

Stew Ross

Body to Brain

ALWED

Let me tell you the story of Alwed Jones,
The man who was buried, without any bones,
They slotted him in to his little brown box,
With his shirt, and his tie, and his favourite socks.

For Alwed died, the result of his skill,
By inventing the theory and principil,
Of medical alchemy, his problem to solve,
However his pills were bound to dissolve.

Born of a family, deep in mid Wales,
Chemical Al went way off the rails,
Invented a bomb at the age of fourteen,
But, to make himself taller was Alweds dream.

Pills, and potions, and powders and such,
Poor Alweds brain never wandered that much,
From his personal goal to be tall at last,
He set himself back with his teenage blast.

As time went by, and his skills improved,
Alweds stature remained, little moved,
And the pills and powders became increasingly strong,
PREDICTABLY, something had to go wrong.

And as sure as a cat is a hairy beast,
Alweds bone stretching pills, set out for a feast,
Instead of theoretical elongation,
Alweds bones set about, deterioration.

For what he forgot during pre preparation,
Was no one before in the medical nation,
Had ever succeeded in skeletal stretching,
The end results were never that fetching.

For Alwed reversed the critical masses,
The balance between the salt and molasses,
The carbon and copper and Boron infusion,
Were misrepresented amongst the confusion.

In a downward spiral of cellular size,
Brought about, poor Alweds, skeletal demise,
And at last he died exceedingly thin,
Sad Alwed Jones was nothing but skin.

And through the slot of his little brown box
With his shirt and his tie and his favourite socks,
We say "fare thee well" poor Alwed Jones,
The man who was dying to grow his own bones.

Body to Brain

And as an aside to this terrible story,
Predictive texting, in all its glory,
Whilst typing the letters to spell out Clyde,
Poor Alweds name was lurking inside.

TOLD YOU HE WAS THIN!

Stew Ross

MOTH

Ok moth! It's you or it's me!
I need to use my towel in a moment you see,
For I will have a shower,
And I swear I'll cry foul,
If I'm finished and you're still, lurking here, on my towel.

But you are still there, takin the Mick,
I'll soon shift you with a deft little flick,
You'll fly through the air, If all goes to plan,
You'll alight, helpless, at the base of the pan.

Then my sick bloodlust will be satisfied,
Your liberty withheld,
Without being tried,
And no one will notice the loss of one moth,
Except for me, and perhaps, men of the cloth.

For if I go through with this,
I shall surely be cursed,
And my gentile aura must certainly burst,
Then I will hang down my sad head in shame,
For drowning you moth, I should accept the blame.

Stew Ross

And all for the sake of the flick of the wrist,
You my powerless friend could scarcely resist,
As you're hurled through the air,
By this human rotter, to meet your demise,
In the foulest of water.

The stewards' enquiry would be most revealing,
And leave little point in this human appealing,
The jury would find, with little confusion,
Twos I, who created this mothy infusion!

Perhaps we would see in the course of my trial,
The pointless nature of broad brush denial,
The defendants' futile pleas of insanity,
This brutal. Moth murdering, scourge of humanity!
Oh! By the way, I was suitably impressed,
As you aqua planed around, with the stroke of your
    breast,
And you changed your style from front crawl to doggy,
Ignoring the impairment of wings flat and soggy.

Body to Brain

So as you complete your lap number ten,
It appeared you were fixing to go round again,
In time it was clear that you had little scope,
To drag yourself onto the high polished slope,
Glazed vitreous sanctuary, courtesy of Shanks,
In moth friendly surface terms,
How lowly it ranks,

At each bold attempt to establish a grip,
Your spindly forelegs just tended to slip,
And you continue along your mindless round trip,
As you think what you'd give
To be rescued by ship, (ship I said),

My conscience is screaming that all this must stop!
To effect your rescue, your wings for to blot,
To reverse this terrible bad luck you've got,
What effort required from me?
Not a lot.

So grabbing some squares of two ply tissue,
I set about resolving your aquatic issue,
Dipping the edge for you to grab hod on,
Quickly the paper turns limp and goes sodden,
And as you swim round to gain your relief,
I'm shocked when you disappear right underneath!

- 15 -

Just when I thought you were no longer mortal,
You emerge round the pan in you flippers and snorkel
Seems troublesome to save a common brown moth,
Moreover with highly absorbent bog cloth!

OK, Now! Attempt number two,
Your time is restricted to remain in this loo,
So please accept this hand of assistance,
It's fatal to maintain this senseless resistance.

Your last chance then, climb on up here,
Let your wings drip dry, as you pull yourself clear,
Success! Mission attained,
I'll leave you just here where the clothes oft are drained
And as you recover, I'll take my shower,
It shouldnae take much more than an hour,

Then when I emerge all clean and refreshed,
I towel myself dry and look for my vest,
And my pants and my shoes and A the rest,
That a man requires for to get dressed,
It's grand the feeling when you're newly washed,
"My God! Wait a moment, my moth I have squashed"
I sat on the drainer, myself for to dry,
And I must have sat on the unfortunate fly,

"I'm sorry my friend, after all we've been through
" I didnae intend, to do this to you"
Now you're impressed upon my bath towel,
It wouldnae be right for me to cry foul.

I'm sure in the night when I should be sleepin,
I can hear the approaching of moth feet creepin,
Your cousins and brothers seeking atonement,
Retribution against me the one, whose bone bent,
The brother that they held close and dear,
That leaves a poor fellow in persistent fear.

I'm sure I'll regret my moth indiscretion,
The incident certainly has left an impression,
This one last thing jumps into my mind,
The last thing that you saw,
Must have been my behind.

What a way to go!

Stew Ross

BISCUIT

Oh! Please can you tell me, have you seen ma biscuit?
Ah went for a pee, and ah thought ah would risk it,
Ah left ma sweet morsel at the side o yon stone,
When ah came back the noo, the stones nae alone!
And noo ahm left searchin, mongst all this rubble,
Ah just hope ma biscuit, is worth all the trouble.

A sweet creation of biscuit and jam,
Second favourite only, to postmen and
    ham,
And now that ma eyes are crossed
    and confused,
Perhaps A'll accept that ma
    biscuit, ah've loosed,
But wait! Great joy and
    ecstatic discovery!
Ahm cock a hoop at ma
    biscuits recovery!

Wait now! This biscuits no mine,
Obviously discarded somewhen doon the line,
Now the quandary A'm in, has left me a dither,
Do ah munch on THIS biscuit, or search here and thither,
From stone to stone all over the yard,
And maybe when ah find it, ma biscuits gone hard,

OR

Do ah settle doon here and recover ma composure,
And reflect on the nature of ma biscuits exposure,
And muse for a while on how rich ah am,
Even though Ah've lost ma biscuit and jam,

But no! It's no use! ah must continue ma search,
If the wife finds Ah've lost it she'll fall off her perch,
Ma life would be hell, biscuit less and grim,
Now WAIT JUST A MINUIT!
There's more in the TIN!!!!!!!!

All Ah need do is sneak past whilst she's sleepin,
And if she wakes up A'll say that I've eaten,
The biscuit she gave me not an hour before,
Ah could not admit that ah lost on the floor,
The biscuit she slaved so hard to create,
Ah know! A'll tell her the biscuit was great!!!

So great in fact ah could do with anither,
"Your baking is almost as good as ma mothers"
OOYA!!!!! " that hurt, what was that for?"
"Why are you throwing my collar and bowl out the door?"
Ah merely intended to compliment your cooking,
And go so far as to say you're good looking,
And snuggle down together; you know what ah mean,
But somehow now, you don't seem all that keen,

Come now lass, you know, you're ma favourite pooch,
And ah love your collar sense, although slightly butch,
A'm asking you now to forgive my indiscretion,
Indulge ma biscuit passion, and get some fresh in,

OK! OK!
Ah can tell by your scowlin, you're a wee bit tetchy,
And about to start howlin,

Body to Brain

Ah didnae mean tae imply you're a terrible cook,
FINE! I'm leavin....right now!.................. Look!

"TORTIS"

Missing, one tortoise, undoubtedly dead,
Affectionately, now formerly, referred to as Fred,
Join with me as I lower my head, and reflect on Freddy,
And the life that he led.

Born in a nest amongst seventy six others,
Mostly sisters but three of them brothers,
All of them rastafarites, idealistic when drunk,
Partial to weed and the odd bit of skunk.

As he got older it was harder to tell,
Save for the size of his beak, and the rings of his shell,
The age of poor Freddie not that it counts,
When you're removed, amongst others in horrific
    amounts,

From your paradise islands, Galapagos,
The raiders and traders could scarce give a toss,
There's brass to be gleaned, spoils to be shared,
The demise of the species, as if they cared!

Body to Brain

And so in a bag and a box and a boat,
Memories of home became more remote,
Thrust into a new world, poor Freddy arrived,
One of the miniscule few who survived.

Mourning his sisters and one of his brothers,
Unaware of what became of the others,
Fred was installed in a glass fronted cage,
Alone, consumed by amphibious rage.
Along came a client, believed they'd done well,
Persuading Fred to come out of his shell,
When clearly Fred had revenge on his mind,
Clamped his beak on this punters behind!
With a hideous yelp, ran to its mother,
This pseudo, would be animal lover.

For a while at least Fred was at rest,
Cocooned in his shell, remote from the test,
Reflecting on how helpless his new situation,
Trying to gauge the deterioration,
Of claws, scales, sharpness of beak,
When his attention was drawn by an intriguing squeak.

"Excuse me please, is there any one in?"
"Are you dead!, or do you just have very hard skin?"
"What's that you say? You're inside your shell?"
"How's a para mousic likely to tell?"
"I swear you have symptoms of rigor mortis!"
"There's no mention here in my book bout a Tortis!"

TORTIS..(Noun)....... hard scaly beast,
In terms of speed has achieved the least,
Beak of steel, cold beady eyes,
Consumes an enormous amount for it's' size,
If you're a hare as soon as you meet it,
You'll assume in a race that you're destined to beat it,
Be wary my friend Tortisnae concluded,
They travel much quicker with their legs extruded.

Back to the story, on meeting the mouse,
Fred cautiously emerges from within his house,
After some initial introductory banter,
Fred concluded Para mousic was a bit of a ranter,
A wee skinny mammal that just couldn't stop,
Another fine inmate of the pets' r us shop.

Body to Brain

Arrived the day, Fred's sold to an owner,
A portly chap with a wife called moaner,
At least that's what Fred often gleaned,
As the portly chaps reference to her as it seemed,
Boy! Could she talk, mostly complaining,
A product of all her mothers good training.

These two had a daughter, trained as a nurse,
Completing poor Freddie's domestic curse,
She was a horror, uncouth and fickle,
Known for attacking her pets with a sickle,
So Fred's course of action became crystal clear,
As soon as tortoisely possible, to escape from here!

As darkness descended, although his task was immense,
Fred dug an escape hole towards the ring fence,
For Fred it was a simple task to discard,
The spoil from his excavations in the exercise yard,
Concealing the earth in the voids of his shell,
Distracting the commandant as the soil did expel,

As the project developed and the tunnel advanced,
Fred realised the air supply should be enhanced,
So with bean can, pop sticks and a few rubber bands,
He assembled a machine to meet respiratory demands,
As the distance increased, with the passage of time,
Fred increased his efficiency by installing a line,
A simple wood cart with a system of ropes,
A true stroke of genius for amphibious folks.

Although roof falls caused Fred palpitations,
He became more convinced by his calculations,
That the fence grew near and escape was believable,
Proof positive that the commandant was deceivable.

His mind was set, the tunnel complete,
With cautious anticipation he took to his feet,
Forming a suitable lump in his bed,
A straw filled effigy of our hero Fred.

He stole to the cupboard where the tunnel began,
And started the air supply according to plan,
On reaching the shaft for the vertical push,
He found himself tangled in a gooseberry bush,

Although clear of the fence, on this darkest of nights,
He was still in the clutches of the security lights,
As the P.I.R detected his movement,
Fred considered his predicament, could use some improvement,
As the guard dog awoke all snarely and crabbit,
He shot straight passed Fred in pursuit of a rabbit,

Freddy emerged from the bush in disbelief,
Shuddered, recalling the size of those teeth,
Gratefully accepting spontaneous distraction,
Fred seized the moment and sprang into action!......
    SLOWLY!

Skirting the flower beds down by the pond,
Negotiating the gravel, the path and beyond,
It seemed clear now as freedom beckoned,
Escape seemed possible just as Fred reckoned,

Unlike his hero who escaped on a scrambler,
A more sedate exit lay in store for our rambler,
It was clear Fred could not play, base ball,
Since they don't make catchers gloves quite that small,
And luckily as Fred avoided the cooler,
He looked forward to life, satisfying and fuller.

So reads the poster: - "has any one seen Fred?"
We hope, but we fear that he, may be dead,
As for us dear reader we understand,
There are thousands of Fred's living throughout this land,
Misplaced warriors from far distant shores,
Reluctant travellers to exotic pet lovers' doors.

Forced to escape, a new life to forge,
Cousins', relations of old lonesome George,
At the end I suppose there must be some hope,
If only somehow one Fred could elope,
And navigate back, to Galapagos,
There to avert this criminal loss,

Somewhen down the line must lay a solution,
Or we must surely face retribution,
There's method in habitats becoming a home,
Let's live our own lives and leave George alone!

Body to Brain

NO FAN OF GARDENING!

Two leaves swirled and fluttered,
In a dance of immanent destruction,
Branches drawn in and spewed,
On the governors instruction,
Grass and weeds trimmed and hacked,
In the name of shape and form,
Nature's progress thwarted,
Since the day that it turned warm.

Body to Brain

- 31 -

Stew Ross

TELEPATHIC INBOX

A moment please whilst I consult my telepathic inbox!
Your enquiry suggests some transfer of information,
But not to me!

You chastise my inactivity,
But I fail to understand that media as an accepted form
    of communication,
This is a modern world but as yet I don't believe we have
    perfected thought transfer.

Therefore please accept my non conformity,
My apparent resistance to comply with your demands,
I may appear of no use to you,
A pinch point, a foil in your flow plan
Disrupter of blue sky thinking, so deep dive that thought!

But then my telepathic inbox was, empty!

PEREGRINE FUDGE

A short intimation for Peregrine Fudge,
Worldwide exponent of shovelling sludge,
Bacterial inspector of gaseous escapes,
Orator of tantalizing sanitary japes,

Teller of stories, sayer of soothes,
Cleaner of Shanks filled porcelain booths,
Waster of bleach, polishing copper,
Council convenience quarry tile mopper,

Peregrine Fudge, man on the edge,
Storing his teeth on a cubicle ledge,
Knocking them off, into the pan,
Tasty distraction for sanitary man,

Developed immunity, odours from hell,
Scourge of community, devilish smell,
All in the course of a days operation,
Unsung hero of an uncaring nation,

Happy at work, Peregrine Fudge,
Worldwide exponent of shovelling sludge.

Body to Brain

Stew Ross

"WELL THAT'S GOT TO COME OFF FOR A START !!!"

CARDIOLOGY

Excuse me nurse could you please scratch ma nose,
For I can't move ma arms, it's too far for ma toes,
And could you please tell me what you have done with
    ma clothes,
Here!! These surgical sheets would make practical throws!

To wind up here has taken some skill,
Beer fags and curry, that's the usual drill,
If I'd changed the balance would ah still be this poorly,
I shouldnae be here! They've got the wrong man! Surely!

Oh but alas they're right! An ahm under the knife,
Paying the price for a fun packed life,
Still, forty odd years an just one blocked pipe,
Ah suppose there's no much justifiable reason tae gripe,

So then dae your worst Mr. Cardiology,
What's that on yer badge? "Acting head of urology!"
Ahm here for repair of a cardiac lesion,
You appear to be working on ma far nether region!

Ma hearts up here, look! Miles from ma crotch,
Is that really ma insides?
Ahm no sure ah can watch!

Stew Ross

COBBLERS TO CATERPILLARS

Caterpillar blues whilst purchasing shoes,
Is quite a conundrum to face,
Because, multiple pairs of same size slippers,
Are all but impossible to trace,

Therefore compromise spurs inventive solution,
And a third of the slippers are bought,
A Technique is developed by arching his back,
Utilising all of the slippers he's got,

For every third set of stumpy short legs,
Are clad in pedestrian apparel,
For our caterpillary friend has learned how to bend,
And is no longer over the barrel............of,

Our friendly cobbler who was rubbing his hands,
At the prospect of significant sales,
A slippery boom! That which swelled his coffers,
Increased his prospects of retirement to Wales,

Abimalech Davies, a Jewish cobbler,
Son of a swine herd from Porth,
Had dreamed of his fortune and some such customer,
Since arriving int city from t north,

Body to Brain

But just as the sale seemed a foregone conclusion,
The bending technique ensued,
And although quite absurd, cut his sale to a third,
Of the record breaking sale that it could……….Be,

Abimalech inhaled and issued forth,
An eloquent sales pitch and oration,
Designed to bemuse and _present_ his shoes,
IRRESISTABLY, to the shoe buying nation,

Although his mark was one third part convinced,
His job remained two third parts undone,
This served to spur our cobbler on,
To complete what the caterpillar begun,

"Honestly sir!" "You're all out of kilter,"
"Your clad feet all appear rather odd,"
"You need to complete the set for your feet,"
"Don't be like a miserable sod"

"You must invest in the shoes for the rest,"
"I shall continue until you give in,"
"If you persist to resist, your arm I shall twist,"
"To miss some of your feet is a sin"

"Can you imagine the look on a prospective wives face?"
"When she observes the state of your clobber"
"I'd be mortified at a later date as I learned,"
"That you blame t'all on your cobbler,"

"SO sir, I must most strongly insist,"
"That you purchase the rest of your boots,"
"For the sake of your wife, for the sake of MY pension,"
"To save the embarrassment of your future off shoots."

"Then I shall retire, but your tires shall be new,"
"And your journey will just have begun,"
"And one day you shall sit with your shoe shining kit,"
"An tell all of this tale to your son,"

"Two hundred and thirty five pounds and ten "p""
"You can have the dubbing and spare laces entirely on me"

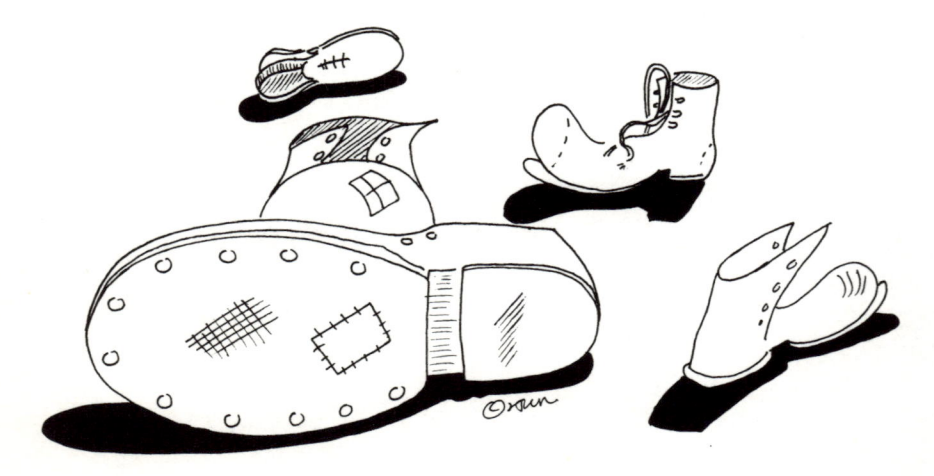

Body to Brain

Stew Ross

SIGNAGE

Note to self, to remind me that I am human,
Created equal, every bit as valuable as these people!
I'm sure they are confused,
They seem to have forgotten that there are others here,
Of similar worth,

The indifference in their faces implies,
That my first impressions were perceptive at least,
"The non caring carers"
It seems that working in this noble profession,
Entered into with gusto, idealism,
Produces a sub race, minds homogenised,
Conditioned to the leisurely pace of this cumbersome
    beast,
How does anything get done around here?

The poor demented creatures milling round this
    labyrinth,
Troll the myriad of corridors seeking the elusive,
Cardiac investigation clinic...........In vain,
And the woman in pinc nez from administration,
Declares with doubtless efficiency, "I shall make a note!"
We, the demented, are left in no doubt, the problem will
    persist.

The opportunity to make a difference passes and fades
    into the ether,
Like countless other enlightenments,
Condemned to the clipboard back catalogue, archived!
Perhaps beside the skeletal remains of our fellow
    labyrinthian,
Misdirected victim, of the signage.

GRADUATE

When a young man or woman graduates,
Their superiors may have the measure of them,
For a while,
And when the drinking is done,
And the dying embers of the celebration fade,
Their achievements, all be they great,
Suddenly seem less significant,
For they have only gained a ticket,
The right to stand in line with countless other fine
    academicals,
And so the game begins.

Endless approaches, mindless presentations,
Analysis in great detail of dress sense,
Latest blue sky thinking, trends,
Now the bright young things strut their stuff,
Preen their feathers, spout their rhetoric,
Carefully prepared, woefully inadequate,
And the corporate monsters listen with disinterest,
Casually probing, waiting for some hint of life,
Priming themselves to pounce on those that show feist.

The bright ones begin to doubt the strength of,
Their mighty, curriculum vitae,
It wasn't supposed to be like this!

A few of the illuminated, although disappointed,
Form their own allegiances,
Become the new corporatehood,
The next generation to scan, to consume, to mould the biddable,
Unaware, perhaps forgotten, their own path,

So what of the nearly, the also ran?
Fading from the light of their glorious moment,
Succumbed to a life of almost,
A catalogue of lost ideas litter the growing free time space in their minds,
So close then, what was amiss?

Prudence

Jimmie's got his name tag back to front,
He's got his mouthpiece in his ear,
His only razor blade is blunt,
He goes down hill in second gear,

He saved some cash from Johnny's shot,
His conscience clear of sins,
His prudence served to fill the cot,
Since his wife produced …..twins!

Farewell to an old friend

I imagined you and I were destined for Valhalla,
Homogenised by circumstance,
You the cruel mistress, I the willing Viking slave,
But like so many who went before me,
My stewardship must end,
No longer custodian, curator, confidant or friend,

Those Arun wavelets no longer kiss your carvel lips,
And for the last time I hear your heartbeat,
Press on towards Littlehampton's slips,
 I tear myself away and as the rope walk bends,
I turn in sad reflection at the way our friendship ends,
And there your majestic silhouette against West Sussex
   sky,
I bid farewell sweet "Themlyay"
From my heart, my soul, just, I.

Body to Brain

Prince of Darkness

So what's the deal with you locked in your room,
Avoiding the light? Do you worship the moon?
Your demeanour suggests impending doom,
Could you be the Prince of darkness?

The way in which you, just appear,
Fills us mere mortals full of fear,
Although not visible, you're often near,
Gauging, casing, monitoring the mood,

On the rare occasion that we meet,
My suspicious inkling becomes complete,
Your furtive eyes, face, white as sheet,
Tight lipped concealment, of the fangs?

You're just off out! It's just dark out!
Our day draws to a close,
Twilight brings with it an awakening, a stirring!
You disappear out into the gloom,
We are left to contemplate,

Body to Brain

What mischief is performed?
What terror? Which sorry soul succumbs
To your complex web of deceit?
What becomes of your life partners,
Debutantes, disappearants,   food?

You seem to survive on little but air,
What sustenance can be gleaned?
What comfort can be taken there?
A liquid lunch at midnight,
Met again in the smallest room before dawn.

It

Now we live in a screwed up world,
Procedure driven,
Slaves to the meeting trail,
Some willing, most confused,
We return home to our hutches, dissatisfied,
And the point was?

Today we didn't make anything,
We didn't solve anything,
We did however, talk a lot,
Talk cannot be cheap,
Check out the wages bill,

When did "work" loose its meaning?
We should change it to "talk",
So, who did you say you "talk" for?
I'm off to "talk" dear,

Body to Brain

Whilst we talk about it,
Who is doing anything about it?
Can any of us remember what, it, was?
When the game is over,
How long would it be before we realise,
We forgot to make money!
Then we will see,
That was IT!!!!!!!!!!!!!!

Memory Foam

Can it be that memory foam cannot lie?
That would indeed make it dangerous stuff,
What would it remember?
What would it regurgitate, and when?
Tortuous uncertainty, until at length,
You collapse into your bolt hole bed,
Only to discover you don't fit!!!!!

Body to Brain

Stew Ross

The Delivery Man

It's nine forty five in the fore noon,
The dogs are both tethered and calm,
From a side door enters a tall man,
Having first parked his shiny white van,
He announced he had a delivery,
And his face cracked a wry kinda grin,
"Whilst I delivered it to your pavement,
I'll be damned (f*****) if I'll bring it in!!!!!!"

On Balance

I met you in the spring time,
I thought how you stood tall,
Now you don't look so marvellous,
As we approach the fall,
Your left eye droops alarmingly,
There's sadness within your eyes,
And a sudden realisation,
That you have grown to reach that size,

Your wit and charm have left you,
Morose and far less jolly,
Things could have been so different though,
If you'd put less in your trolley,
It may be that I'm being unfair,
On reaching this assumption,
But I'm more than likely right you're plagued,
By over zealous munchin!

Body to Brain

It's sad to think that in times past,
You stood proudly by my side,
Now it seems you're more inclined,
To slope away and hide,
Lass, the solution is clear,
And well within your grip,
If you don't stop eating jaffa cakes,
For sure the scales will tip,
 And not in your favour.

Stew Ross

Frog

If God was a frog and your mother was toast,
Of what would the rest of us have to boast?
And if your dad was a pig in a very bad wig,
How could we possibly eat Sunday roast?
Then all of us vegetarians would be,
Unless, of course, Michael Fish came to tea.

Body to Brain

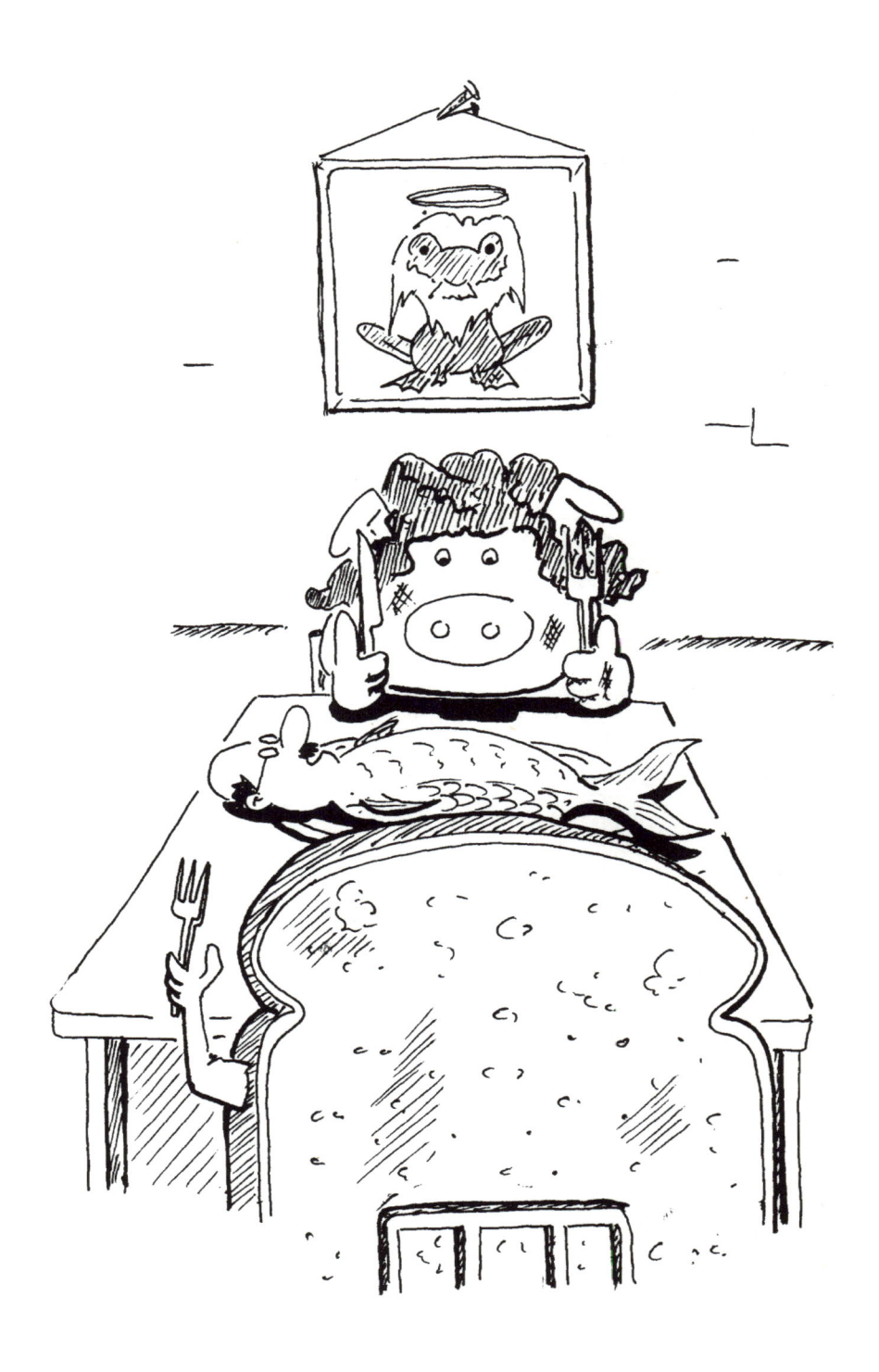

Stew Ross

OK Hamster…….OK

You made the mistake, and you paid the price,
But you find that your ears are still burning,
Long after your hamster has turned up its toes,
You find that its wheel is still turning,

The rhythmic squeak consumes your mind,
At the cost of peaceable slumber,
What a desperate weight to carry around,
Such guilt with which to encumber.

The Process

A perfectly formed floater,
Staring right back at me,
The result of an internal process,
On things I consumed for my tea,

A fascinating transformation,
On my regular meat and two veg,
But can someone offer explanation,
Why they sometimes get stuck round the edge?

I muse at my floaters persistence,
And I wonder just how to get rid,
And come to the ultimate conclusion,
Walk away! And close down the lid!

Body to Brain

Massacre

Cold still eyes scream shock and surprise,
No time to reflect as the spirit dies,
Could it be no one heard your cries?
As your Wednesday came to an end,

Whilst Cumbria's peelers tally the score,
Contorted bodies communicate no more,
Conclude their business on a northern floor,
Who is left to explain?

M.O.T

Today my car endured its latest m.o.t,
And the engineer presented this report unto me:-
But I don't understand a word of it you see,
It's above and beyond comprehension,

Apparently my wishbone is missing a bush,
And the nearside compensating valve has worked loose,
I may as well put my head in the noose,
And enquire as to the engineers' intention,

I feel sure he will charge me copious amounts,
As once before I fell foul of this garages' accounts,
At length I lose my nervousness and resilience surmounts,
My fear to ask the fateful question,

"Excuse me sir" begins my tentative enquiry,
As I recall the engineer to be notoriously fiery,
And objects to people challenging his word,
Having killed several people for less, I have heard,

"I'd like to enquire and hoped you'd explain,"
"Why my poor car has failed its m.o.t once again,"
"Has my mode of transport just gone down the drain?"
"And should I plan alternative arrangements?"

In response to my question the engineer cracked a grin,
And sharply drew quantities of oxygen in,
"Well it's really a debate about where to begin"
"And I'm not sure you can handle the reality"
"For a start your brakes should be filled with dot 4"
"As they don't make the glycerol based product no more"
"And since I found your left side brake pads on the floor"
"I predict an immanent fatality"

"If you come down by here I Am sure you will see"
"A dull yet discernable reflection of you and of me"
"As you're tyre groove is zero whilst the minimum is three"
"A fact I can scarce overlook"

"Regarding the amount of ferrous oxide"
"On the A and the B posts and all down the near side"
"And the floor no longer divides the in from outside"
"The mere fact you are here is a fluke"

"There is considerable play in the steering rack"
"Which could cause your car to prescribe an entirely random track"
"I don't know how you got here, but you're not going back,"
"With my blessing nor with my condonement"

"And if in an emergency you were to be found"
"Your horn could not emit any sound"
"As the coil has burned out and has gone down to ground"
"Perhaps now is the time for atonement"

"Moreover if something unforgiving you were to strike"
"You could well find yourself impaled on a spike"
"As the steering wheel nut is as rotten as you like"
"And would fail in the course of the impact"

"I agree you would no doubt be safe"
"If your seat belt material had not started to chaff"
"I really do admire the extent of your faith"
"And marvel at how you are intact"

"To surmise Mr Jones, your car is a wreck"
"It's a miracle you have not yet broken your neck"
"And the fuel you have used must have given OPEC"
"A false impression of demand"

"My advice to you is make use of your shoes"
"And find alternative transport"
"Please get into you head, your Jalopy is dead!"
"I cannot issue a new safety passport!"

Stew Ross

This was a somewhat brutal appraisal of my beloved car,
My faithful "voiture" who has brought me thus far,
Who was this man who cast such aspersions?
I will not give up; rather I will seek more opinions,
Only less expensive ones!

Angel's Kiss

Today I was truly humbled by an angel's golden kiss,
One she was unaware of, or ever could she miss,
What beauteous compassion from such a troubled mind,
Such innocent generosity,
Leaves the rest of us behind.

Time Lord

He's a corporate time lord,
A stickler for the rules,
A scrutineer of clock cards,
Punched in by us poor fools,

In his antique police box,
He travels through the week,
Catching whispers on the breeze,
Inciting gossip from the meek.

Body to Brain

Gressive

One day you'll cross swords with a Gressive,
Cause Gressives are surely abound,
In remote neuks and crannies,
That's where Gressives are found,

With their short stumpy legs,
And their pock marked skin,
And a singular hair,
Sticking out from their chin,

I would not recommend fighting Gressives,
As you're bound to come off second best,
Perhaps you should pick someone your own size,
If you need to get stuff off your chest.

Body to Brain

Stone Face

You stand alone with your stone face,
Your sticky out eyes and your lip out of place,
You seem to have a problem with the human race,
I'm not sure how you can blame me,

You catch my eye when I'm least aware,
And I'm captured by your tractor beam stare,
And the distance foreshortens from here to there,
As you attempt to take over my mind,

Realising the danger I put up defences,
I tune in to otherwise redundant senses,
And foil your attack with one of my own,
Take some of that! You hideous crone!

With your hunched up shoulders, and you fierce pointed nose,
You exude unhappiness from your head to your toes,
Your demeanour could only be described as morose,
"Being so happy" is what keeps you going,

Body to Brain

If you coughed there's no doubt, it would probably hurt,
And I am sure you are wearing your very last shirt,
But don't look at me like I'm some piece of dirt,
Your pain was not caused by me,

I only came in to buy a tin,
Of beans and a bottle of best value gin,
It seems you consider my actions a sin,
If your face gives a true reflection,

I'm glad you occupy the adjacent aisle,
And there's distance between myself and your bile,
Is it beyond hope that one day you'll smile?
Perhaps I should just dream on.

Stew Ross

Summer Breeze

Summer breeze wafting promise of fine repast,
Tantalise taste buds, excite gastric memories of the past,
Salivate in anticipation,
"H" was carried away by his culinary fantasy,
And Jose the Spanish waiter thought to himself,
"He eees out to lunch!"

Luscious Lucy

Luscious Lucy lives her life in lycra enhanced tights,
She has to pat the price for all those beer and curry nights,
Her arse is not a shapely form, with a random abstract plight,
Protruding through peripherals, plagued by cellulite,

Lucy lives the Lycra dream and jogs on down the road,
Having first applied lubrication,
For fear she might explode.

Ode to a Prostitute

Owed to a prostitute, one complimentary ticket,
To investigative clinics for diseases of the wicket,
For she encumbers punters with something quite
    unsavoury,
Sick revenge for her life, within sexual slavery,

Her sad mind bent by drug misuse,
Employed to dull the pain,
Fuels the need to feed the beast,
And to turn the tricks again.

The Watchers at the wall

From obscure neuks and hidden crannies,
Upon my bed and at my grannies,
All around my pristine home their beady eyes won't leave
    alone,
This long suffering up keeper of the fight,
The vacuum was not enough,
The fine grade filter not the rough,
Deployed to no avail.

Having dodged cyclonic
    power,
Perhaps met their final
    hour picked up by bristle,
Only to usurp the pan,
These slippery characters
    amass in cracks and
    crevices,
Awaiting opportunity but in
    the meanwhile we co
    exist,
A stand off ensues……..

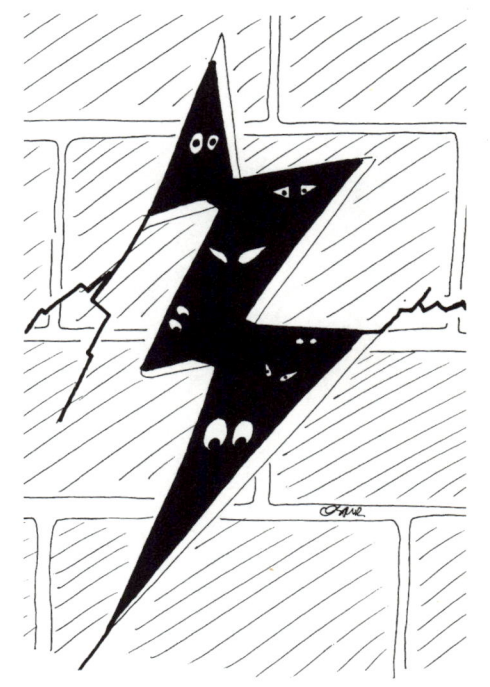

The conditioned fabric of the gown,
I gratefully wrap around my freshly showered body,
May play host to countless passengers of the Mitey kind,
I may suspect, but then I don't suspect,
And I bask in blissful luxurious ignorance,
Conductor of the "gown town train",

The lazy breeze provides the vector,
Driven by oil filled convector, the highway to the sky,
The means by which the critters fly,
Whilst those not out manoeuvred by nasal defences,
Lodge deep in alveoli, nestling, irritating,
Coagulate into damaging mass,
Hideous microscopic travellers through blind and rug,
The watchers at the wall.

Body to brain

Body to brain, are you receiving me? Hello!!!!!
Is there any body up there?
Caw typical! Just as I suspected sleeping on duty again,
Oi mate! I'm getting more than a bit ticked off,
Carrying you around all day whilst you lollop around,
In you cranial soup, pontificating,
Do us a favour, snap to it and give us a clue,
What you want us to do for you, oh almighty one!

Whilst you've been "out to lunch",
We have had a troublesome incident in the "plumbing department"
Dyna Rod are now on the highest state of alert,
And all cleaning staff leave is suspended forthwith,
This may come as a complete surprise to you,
However we consider that you have taken your eye off the ball,
Consequently you have compromised the status quo within our biosphere,
We don't want to end up like the other brainless cretins,
So how about it? Shake a leg, you have the power, or do you?

Stew Ross

You can't really decide to go for a stroll,
Make a brew, prepare a roll,
Not without the rest of us being compliant,
So who really holds the power in this relationship?
Your future sir, Is under review!

Body to Brain

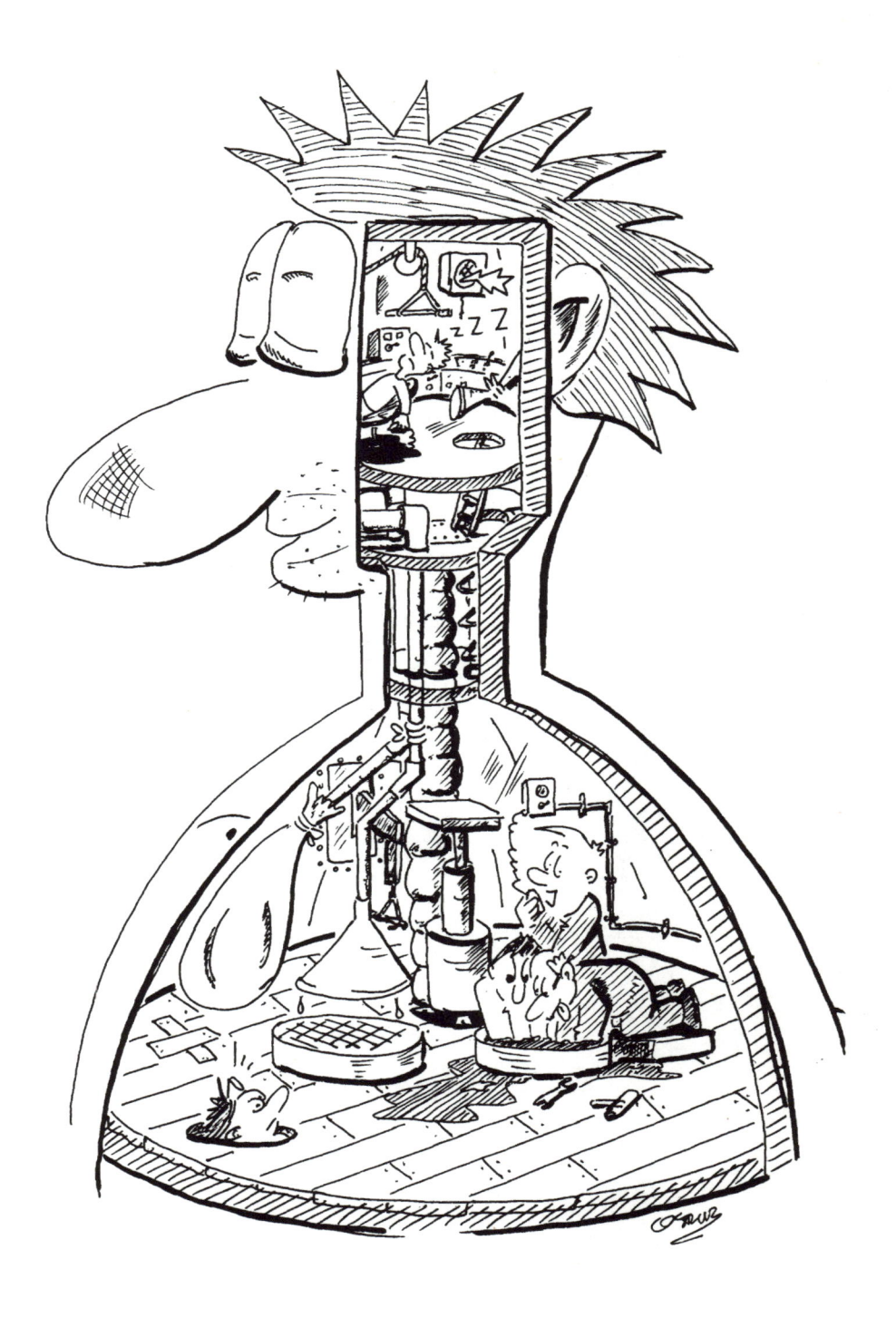

Stew Ross

Canteen

In the canteen of life we sit in collective isolation,
Holding individual silent counsel,
Perhaps previous generations would indulge,
By ribbing each other with subliminal jaunty japes,
But in every sense, this lot are struck dumb,

Wait a moment! I don't speak in subliminal tones either,
Perhaps I am the only one here in isolation,
No.....I rather feel my first impression was a good one,
Trying to find life behind my fellow diners' eyes proves
    pointless,
There may well be lights on, but there is no one home.

Chicken

So, what drives a fresh young chicken down the oven
    ready route?
How was that notion sold? Just how was the concept
    put?
"You'll go far, at least feed a family of six"
Dear mother used to tell us when we were only chicks,
Could we have understood what fate she had in mind?
Up to which hideous contract had we unwittingly signed?

Would I have signed had I known the bag I'd end within?
Would I have welcomed the prospect of being pressed into
    a tin?
I'm not sure my giblets were designed to make a brew,
A gravy to compliment the grub that feeds your motley
    crew,
If you don't mind I'd like to keep my bits and parts
    together,
I rather like the feeling I am afforded by my feather, and
    all its neighbours!

No frosty ending will I have! No polystyrene platter!
No injections underneath my skin to make out that I'm fatter!
I shall live my life as God himself decreed,
And I shall not rest till all of chicken kind is freed,
I shall be a poultry revolutionary, with substantial pluck,
I shall disable transport networks, cripple supply chains, with luck,

And all my fellow chickens will champion the cause,
I shall live to revel in the clutches of their applause,
With luck I will rise to top the pecking order,
Preen strut and scratch amongst the best hens in the border,
In terms of avian importance, there is a difference I must beg,
Twix your ordinary and your organic free range egg,

It's not just in the size, nor the colour of the yolk,
It's in the jaunty way, in which its offspring tells a joke,
Whilst flocking, socialising, grubbing out the tucker,
Amusing fellow walkabout's like that antipodean plucker,
A three legged chick who hailed from lands down under,
I'm sure that given half a chance he'd cast our foes asunder,
But wait! Could it be it's all a dream? And I'm sold for a poultry sum,
Destined to be a Sunday roast with Paxo stuffed up my neck!

Peni Pads

Come on lads gather round I'll tell yees all a story,
The likes of which you've never read, nor heard on Jackanory,
A story of a secret all the lasses have been keeping,
A story of an invention that stops yer bladder leakin,
A story that's only for the lads, no ifs, no buts, no maybes,
And if you want to listen in we charge tenner ladies!

Now then lasses there's panic in your eyes,
We've seen through your subterfuge; cast aside your lies,
For a simple sister has let your secret slip,
The means by which you lasses contain that troublesome drip,
That disconcerting seepage, perplexing exudate,
That leads to moisture in your pants and makes you very late,

Now lads, be honest like, the time for truth is here,
We may have similar problems, blamed it on the beer,
However now we know the answer, plans are duly laid,
We will have our own device to rival every maid,
We've gathered our materials, and measured every size,
For comfort, ease of fitting, and the speed at which it dries,

At last we have the prototype and testing shall begin,
Marketing design the box to put the product in,
A campaign of espionage ensues to spread the rumour,
And blokes begin to wonder why they hadn't seen one sooner,
Suddenly a ground swell of interest spreads throughout the land,
Retail pressure builds with the insatiable demand,

Finally then the launch date, release to great aplomb,
Blokes arrived from near and far to try the product on,
An instant revolution turned many fellows' heads,
Saving embarrassing explanations for moistness in their beds,
The inventors of the product gained critical acclaim,
But the managing director could not reveal its name,

They held a competition to find its nom de plume,
The nature of the product however left the entrants little room,
A lad from Esher London penned the killer blow,
The perfect product tag as can be seen below:-
It may have cost a tenner ladies and now for all the lads,
We'll catch the drips within our hips with brand new "Peni Pads".

Slim   ?

A rotund young lassie came a waddling by,
And I noticed that she had a tear in her eye,
"Come now lass, try nae tae cry",
"For things aye get better in the end, bye and bye",

Tell me now, what's your affliction?
I bet you've got a mars bar addiction,
Jings lass!!! You've a hell o a power,
Ma knees turned to jelly at the sight o your glower,

Tell me your name,
Or can you nae divulge,
Perhaps YOU can explain,
The extent of your bulge,

Did you aye get caught?
With yer nose in the barrel,
Did it lead to you wearin this outsize apparel?
Ach! I'm fully aware I should pay you no mind,

But, put quite simply, I'm just no blind,
You're HUGE!!! And you're takin up space,
A generous example,
A slimming disgrace!!!.

Letter to God

For this interruption Lord I must apologise,
But I feel I have information in relation to your demise,
You see, your Gig's on Sunday mornings,
With luck we're all in bed,
Having partied to the wee small hours,
Not really thinking of you, it must be said,

All too soon it's Sunday and we're not very well,
You didn't build too many bridges,
With the ringing of your bell,
Our head beneath the covers,
To somehow hide from all the guilt,
A Sunday morning ritual since the day the Kirk was
    built,

There's crucial information Lord,
Makes my observation complete,
The heathens immerse themselves,
In Omnibuses Coronation Street,
In facing such competition Lord surely you can tell,
Sunday morning seats within your house,
Are proving really tough to sell,

Stew Ross

You could revise the way our eyes,
Lift up to you on high,
You could install within us all,
God fear, on the sly,

But, I much prefer the notion,
That you climb down from your perch,
Reveal yourself to man and beast,
De mystify the search,

Continuance in the present vein,
Will drive your punters out,
And you'll look within collection plates,
To find that you've got nowt!

How then could a potless God,
Expect to fill his dwindling pews,
I feel sure that I would change my ways,
If I were in your shoes,

Therefore Lord if I may make so bold,
And offer some advice,
From this day forth, on wedding days,
You gather up the rice,

Body to Brain

For times ahead look Spartan,
If your word is to survive,
Perhaps a subtle signal,
To let us know that you're alive,

I'm now not sure that your regime,
Can ever be maintained,
Run, as it is, by those men in black,
You know, the ones which you have trained,

It seems to me you've lost control,
Your captains rule the roost,
Maybe they need a refresher course,
To give their faith a boost,

Perhaps a weekend seminar,
Teaching congregational interaction,
Or at least some pointers,
On how to raise the kirks attraction,

Lord I'm trying to avoid on your behalf,
The cost of consultation,
And to raise your profile,
In your publics contemplation,

Stew Ross

But Lord, you have to help yourself,
For I'm just a simple bloke,
And you're my only friend on facebook,
So who else is there for me to poke?

Ambition

Like a dutiful soldier I salute and obey,
Whilst I make mental notes on all that you say,
I will take revenge at the and of the day,
So go ahead, fill your boots with importance,

Stick out your breast more so than the rest,
Be the first past the post,
Impress the rest with heave of your chest,
As you appear to achieve more than most,

Go ahead let us see what you've really got,
I'll bet that it doesn't amount to a lot,
If you fly with the crows then you're bound to get shot,
Still, when did you ever heed friendly warning?

When you finally succumb to the ultimate dive,
And there's no more life saving tales to contrive,
Do you feel that we'll all be glad you're alive?
Or will you just be left standing alone?

As you witness your empire unfold,
What tales of sympathy do you think will be told?
Or will you just firmly be shut out in the cold?
A breakdown or service replacement,

Stew Ross

When you discover yourself deep in that hole,
And you find your staff impossible to cajole,
You'll be left in no doubt as you hear the bell toll,
Your account is prepared and presented,

Before it's too late and you suffer that fate,
A solution is clearly at hand,
Remove a proportion of what's on your plate,
Stop circling!! And come in to land.

Red Haze

He was aware he would have to cross occupied territory,
If he was to stand a chance of making it to his sock
    drawer alive,
So he decamped and snaked around the foot of the bed,
Whilst clinging to his last chance to survive.

For SHE was on the warpath, the worst he had seen yet,
And the overriding mystery was in understanding,
Why, SHE became upset,

Tentative approaches are met with stark hostility,
Little doubt surrounds the nature of her tongues mobility,
As it lashes round his lugs with venomous intent,
Bilious exudate, ill considered, aye, but meant.

Well, he can only assume that some evil mischief is afoot,
That her mind and tongue have been driven,
Down this character assassination route,
The one where negotiated settlement cannot be attained,
That could leave the unsuspecting negotiator emotionally
    maimed,

Perhaps it would be better then to remain silent,
Subservient, in the interest of self preservation,
For hopefully calm will return in a few days,
When an altogether more pleasant character will emerge,
From the red haze.

Fat

Wherever she goes I have little doubt her belly will arrive first,
Her friends remove all sharp objects for fear that she may burst,
As she travels she is pre empted by her belly,
This troublesome blob that interrupts her turning off the telly,

So rolling back defeated, resigned to viewing more,
She munches cakes and mourns the loss of things now on the floor,
For several years the carpet has been sorely out of reach,
Since she indulged and took on, the mantle of a peach,

And now she views dropped items from afar:-
The telly changer, her newest false teeth, the tax disc from her car,
Her friends no longer visit; she bides here all alone,
Isolated, devastated, nearly forty stone,

Her shopping is done on line, deposited on the hallway floor,
Dragged in by hook of walking stick, since she can't squeeze through no more,
She has become a prisoner in a cell without defence,
A victim of her expansion, now that she is so immense,

And yet she keeps on eating, stuck within the loop,
Scoffing fondant fancies and mulligatawny soup,
A lethal combination, a very rocky road,
Will likely cause her one day, to spontaneously explode,

But would she pass unnoticed? Would the explosion make a sound?
How long would it be before her bits and parts were found?
What of the investigation? What conclusion would be reached?
What reason could be found as to why her skin was breeched?

A terrible realisation that she died within this hovel,
And took her final journey on a crime scene investigators shovel.

Body to Brain

The Marked Man

The tale of a marked man,
Tattooed on the sole of his foot,
Who stamped on doubt relentlessly,
From the inside of his boot,

A confident man who'd little regard,
For vexing questions whether diverse or hard,
Exuding confidence, on much knowledge he draws,
If only he knew what the question was,

The mark of enquiry lies at the heart of his sole,
Leaving him curious to understand,
Which part he is of the whole,

Life's journey offers up little explanation,
The tattoo simply, a pre preparation,
A question mark to his very existence,
Testimony to his nature, his inquisitive persistence,

When finally one day his sole is laid bare,
An unanswered question mark,
Will be found under there,
A reminder of solutions not yet found,
Nor will be by him, now he's under the ground.

Wallaby Dynamics

How does one weigh a young wallaby?
If you can't make the fellow stand steady?
He'll hop all around your bathroom,
And bounce off, before you're quite ready,

You could aye fill the bath full of water,
And bundle your wallaby in,
Catch the overflow with copious towelling,
And then wring it out in a tin,

Then deducting weight of receptacle,
You'd be left with a liquid amount,
But can someone resolve the conundrum,
Does internal Wallaby gas count?

For this surely contributes to displacement,
And therefore overall mass,
I would hate to insult a poor wallaby,
On account of some hideous gas,

Can you offer a practical solution?
Which I can present to the zoo,
I only a simple consultant,
Although quite complex calculations I'll do,

Stew Ross

It's ten o'clock in the forenoon,
And I'm munchin a pack of rich tea,
I'll trust in divine inspiration,
And hope that an answer will jump out at me,

Presently all that is jumping,
Is my furry marsupial friend,
In order to save my reputation though,
I will weigh this beast in the end !!........ SO

Clutching a bag from the market,
I pounce, and envelop its head,
I'm not fooled by its inactivity,
By the way it pretends that it's dead,

I'm aware it's about to start wriggling,
And conscious that my plan isn't great,
So I phone up the zoos directors,
To inform them, that my estimate is late.

Body to Brain

Stew Ross

The shop assistant

The shop assistant slouched unattractively,
Against the Carpigiani ice cream maker, ruminating,
At length she stirred, having realised, I presume,
That she had some function to perform,
If only she could recall what that was,

I relent unexplainably and resort to offering clues:-
"A mug of coffee please" I bleat,
Whilst searching her eyes for some hint of percipience,
Only to be met by the epitome of incomprehension,

"You haven't worked here long have you?"
I challenge, to which she responded,
Issuing forth a nasal titter akin to the sound of a goat,
At last! We were making progress,
And an excuse for her ruminating was found,

Since I don't speak goat, I gave up and went next door
   for a beer.

Stew Ross

Make It Up

You shake up your make up, apply the paste,
For sure, it must be to somebody's taste,
Pencils and teasers to make things curl,
You glue things in place in case they unfurl,

Your movement is constant, a chain of events,
Just think of the embarrassment your action prevents,
With your eyes well defined, outline the blue,
What makes you think someone's looking at you?

Your powder puff, creates the illusion,
Your face is perfection, lights twisted diffusion,
Detracts from the blemishes now covered over,
The impression that everything's coming up clover!

Now you sport your corporate face,
And assume your position in the daily rat race,
No doubt you'll touch up, as the day progresses,
And merge with the others in their uniform dresses,

Pointing out exits fore, aft and mid,
With cherry red lip and dapple grey lid,
You're customer facing, as you strut down the aisle,
But your teeth sport some lipstick, that spoils your smile,

Stew Ross

Well you did get away with the ruse for a minute,
A beautiful dream for the time you were in it,
But we saw the truth at o six thirty one,
Your unadorned canvas, before work began.

Teddy Rock

You stare wistfully into each others eyes,
Seeking out the comfort and solace afforded by your
   friendships bond,
Hand in paw
Together you will face the unknown, silently, tentatively,
Love stronger than general comprehension,
Emerges from the nights clutches triumphantly,
And the day dawns to the cheery sounds,
Of rustling leaves and urgent bird song,

You are oblivious to the other journeymen within the
   <u>uncertain</u> room,
But you do portray the feelings openly,
That others suppress and badge machismo,
The audience looks on quizzically,
Privately envious of your pillar, hugging their pillows,
Reaching out, grasping surrogate pillars of their own,
Whilst into each others eyes you gaze,
And transport each other to happier places,

Hands and paws complete the friendship ring,
And create your protective shield,
Cohorts within the impervious brotherly bond,
A decision is made; you get dressed, and fix to leave,
We're all impressed, and yes, completely envious of your
    impending freedom!
And with your phone clamped to your head,
Still clutching tightly, paw of Ted,
You disappear into the cities hum drum,

So here ends our brief interlude,
You've gone, where only brave men could,
For sure you leave behind reflective thinkers,
You wear your heart upon your sleeve,
And proudly you and Teddy leave,
Now us poor sods must re adjust our blinkers.

Body to Brain

Teach Me

Teach me don't chastise me,
The things within your head,
For they will all be lost,
On the day that you are dead,

Then all your frantic cramming,
Intellectual pursuit,
Will all be lost forever,
How can that be deemed astute?

So teach me don't chastise me,
Take a moment out,
Consider consequences,
Of a put down or a shout,

At the moment you are switched off,
Oblivious unaware,
Woeful in your ignorance,
Of the power of your glare,

Better men have crumbled,
Spirits crushed before your eyes,
Could you detect the nervousness,
In their faltering replies?

Body to Brain

I doubt that you even noticed,
Tight, wrapped up in self esteem,
At which point did you discover,
You're the best there's ever been?

There's many are affected,
By the shadows you have cast,
A few moved on to pastures new,
Free from you at last,

For those still here living half lives,
Anticipate the pain,
When something less than perfect,
Sparks retribution once again,

So teach me, don't chastise me,
Your knowledge you must share,
Show me some compassion,
Some indication that you care,

Credit me with scant intelligence,
Recognise just, a little skill,
Developed before I met you,
Not product of your will,

But alas, you'll never teach me,
Your knowledge will be lost,
Protected by jealous need,
NOT to share at any cost,

What legacy will you bequeath?
That will endure when you retire,
We'll never know for it will disappear,
On the day that you expire.

Body to Brain

CAT & BAT

I'm crouchin' here, on the top of this shelf,
An am feelin kina, pleased wi masell,
Fur ah catched a bat, broucht it intae the room,
Noo ahm watchin it fly, roon, roon,... an roon,

An every time it comes close intae view,
I arch ma back, ma arm fur tae slew,
An a hit it a kick,.... sometimes two,
A most satisfactory game?..............well,
It'll do fur the Noo!

Feline life in this hoos is a scunner,
How ave no lost ma marbles,
Ah can only but wunner,
In order tae amuse, an keep masell sane,
Ah often invent masell a new game,

- 121 -

Ave tried wi a moos, a snail an a rat,
But fur noo ah'll hae tae mak do wi a bat.

Its wee skinny fingers fair tickle ma nose,
How it kens where its goin, well, a'body knows,
An how can it sleep hanging up by its toes,
Och ah think ah'll release it,.... richt noo,...... as it goes,

BUT,

Dinnae tell ma brother, He'll think ave gone soft,
He's younger than me; an he hods me aloft,
If he ever found out that ah let ma bat go,
Ah'm sure that ma image would incur a great blow,

Ah ken wit we'll dae! We'll pretend it expired!,
Seems reasonable tae assume,... that it must hae bin tired,
Fur hours its bin flyin the extent of the room,
Just flyin an flyin, roon roon.......... an roon,

An noo its no there, it fell doon an croaked,
Ma new game ower,
All puggled an choked,
It crawled ower there, jumped oot the flap,
No able to dae the penultimate lap,

So now here Ah sit, in deepest reflection,
Inventin ma story ta aid self protection,
An as fur ma brother, He'll never know,
That Ah captured ma bat, an then let it go.

CORNELIUS

Fare thee well Cornelius Caruthers,
The man with six sisters and twenty five brothers,
And forty eight children by ten different women,
His soldiers of life had no trouble with swimmin!

Alas! He has left us, loosely acquainted,
With his outlook on life and the pictures he painted,
"Cornelius the artist" it said on the door,
We won't see much of his paintings no more.

His brushes and pallet lie idle and still,
His easel hung from a hook on the sill,
A litter of half finished canvass abound,
Lifeless! Without our Cornelius around.

For as an aside and as one of his quirks,
Cornelius would only sign one of his works,
The one with the woman voluptuous and bare,
Reclining seductively, right over there!

Body to Brain

And there it was, during one of their sessions,
She fell foul of, Caruthers impressions,
For Cornelius maintained an extensive collection,
Of molded records of dental correction,
Work done as his dentist insisted,
To re align the hideously twisted!

Gnashers aside and above and beyond,
Affixed themselves securely to this prostrated blonde,
With sudden violent realization,
She ejected herself from her recumbent station,
And with less than a graceful pas de deux,
She impaled her foot on an upturned shoe,

At this point Cornelius dived quickly for cover,
Too late! However, he was squashed by his lover!
And sadly as quickly as life had begun,
Cornelius realized, his race had been run,

On bitter reflection his life on the ebb,
Cornelius considered the style of the web,
That he wove in his years as a desperate letch,
And wondered how much his paintings would fetch,
To support all his children by ten different lovers,
Our champion of activities with under the covers,

And now that Cornelius had come to the end,
Extinguished by t flesh of his portly blonde friend,
A phrase of somewhat perplexing banality,
Brought home to Cornelius, the pressing reality,
And as he succumbed to this fatal blow,
He should have realized "you reap what you sow"

For if he had signed "Cornelius Caruthers",
That may have forewarned these now husbandless
    mothers,
However lets err on the side that is bright,
His antics have given us something to write,
And now as he lies at peace in his grave,
His lineage secured, his prowess displayed,

We must not decry old Caruthers the rude,
Whist fully clothed he painted them nude!
For he never revealed his work on completion,
And he didn't believe in artistic deletion,
Except in the case of their clothes as it goes,
But after his subjects cemented their pose,

So farewell to you, Cornelius Caruthers,
Clothes remover, creator of mothers,
Flattened artists blessed release,
Cornelius Caruthers, God rest you in peace!

Body to Brain

Stew Ross

Lush

Weekend breaks and weekday fixtures,
Drinking experimental mixtures,
To know the cause and gauge effect,
Suggests developed intellect,

Numb the senses addled brain,
But can it really dull the pain?
Of day to day reality,
Keep on drinking, perhaps we'll see.

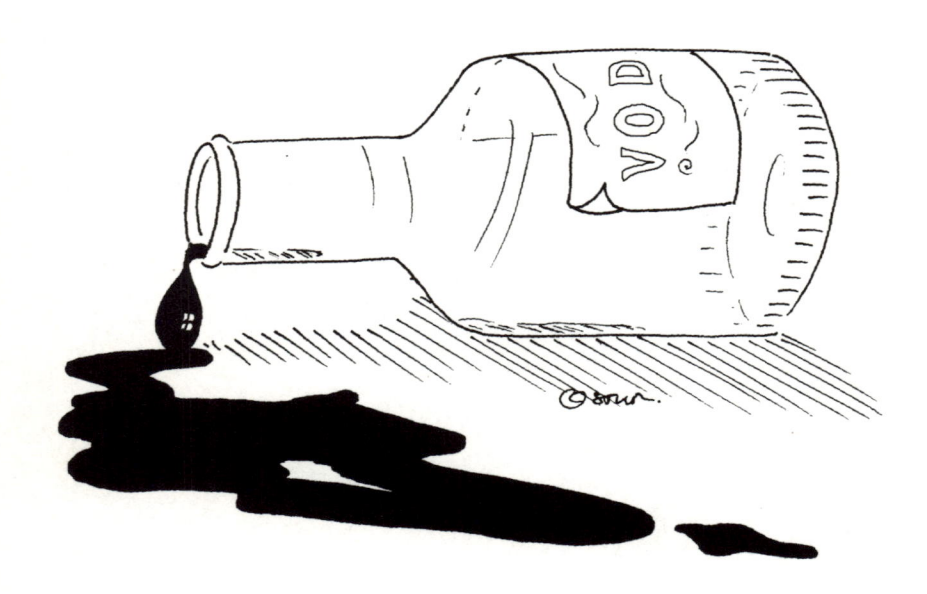

Gin Soaked

I don't really care much for working,
It just gets in my way,
When I have a drink,
I don't tend to think,
How I'm gonna earn a little pay,

Sittin here alone on my front porch,
I got me a bottle of gin,
Of course what would be nice,
If I had a little ice,
And perhaps a slice of lemon to drop in,

Things these days are so damned expensive,
But hey! At least I got my booze,
It makes me feel well,
But no one can tell,
I got gapping holes in ma shoes,

That's alright if it aint rainin,
If it does I will have to stay indoors,
If I run out of gin, I'll need to get some in,
Slope down to seven eleven on all fours,

Stew Ross

That will lead to soggy knee caps,
I could maybe wrap my shoes in plastic bags,
Then shuffle to the store,
Dent my pride some more,
All, for the sake of booze and fags,

So I'll sit and I shall pray for clement weather,
For that would surely save me from my plight,
I know that once I said,
That I would never beg,
The way I feel right now, I just might,

I realise I'm the creator of my situation,
Lord knows how much this man despairs,
Despite my missin wealth,
At least I've got my health,
For that I thank the big fella upstairs,

Things these days are so damned expensive,
But hey! At least I got my booze,
It makes me feel well,
But no one can tell,
I got gapping holes in ma shoes,

Body to Brain

A Mothers Love

She concentrates intently with her head off to one side,
On the stories you invented, and the lies you couldn't
    hide,
Your foolish ramblings let you down,
Your understanding lost,
You spurn her faith and mothers love,
But she don't count the cost,
No she doesn't count the cost,

Mothers love is given freely, conditions don't apply,
No matter what you'll be, she knows one day you'll fly,
You could've made it easier,
Spare her a little thought,
Consumed by your own troubles,
You forgot the things she taught,
You forgot the things she taught, you!,

She cared for you completely, protected you from sin,
Clothed you on the outside, developed the soul within,
But you threw it all back at her,
As if she did you wrong,
Unbeknown to you sir,
She loved you all along,
Yes she loved you all along,

Body to Brain

When you needed refuge, your mother took you in,
Didn't ask too many questions,
Didn't ask you where you'd bin,
Even though she had suspicions,
She parked them in her mind,
She dealt with your conditions,
But then they say that love is blind,

You became reclusive,
Concealed behind closed doors,
You think of mother and her friends as apathetic bores,
You slip out after darkness,
Into the evenings gloom,
There's a stark aire of uncertainty,
Outside the devils room,

Although you left a year ago, your influence still reigns,
You tried to hide but let it show,
It was not just growing pains,
You skulk around dark corners,
With shadows for your friends
You must emerge and face your fears,
Society recommends,

HAS BEEN

He's got a sixty four thousand dollar toothbrush,
The bristles are made out of gold,
It's been his sole and most precious possession,
Since his wife left him out in the cold,

Now he hangs around bars, blagging beds,
Breaking hearts and dodging feds,
He's trying to be the slickest man in town,

His attitudes against him,
His wrinkles let him down,
He's got chat up lines with dents in,
The millionth time around,

But he still insists on trying,
His patter finely honed,
Without defining preference,
For brunette redhead or blonde,

His passion is indiscriminate,
Any port within his storm,
A prospect, and he moves in on it,
She only needs be luke warm,

Body to Brain

Now his sights are set much lower,
More targets are within scope,
Although he has no six pack to show her,
He still expects she'll cope,

With God's gift to female kind,
A badge he proudly wears,
Although now he's slightly blind,
And struggles climbing stairs,

His joints need lubrication,
With oil or wintergreen,
His lifetime of predation,
What was, becomes, has been!

Last Day at the Office.

You take that last note from your inbox,
You face the journey home,
Although surrounded by subordinates,
You find you're all alone,

A final realisation,
you're no better than the rest?
It's time for self analysis,
And to nurse your fallen crest,

"Mrs Jones, our heart felt condolences,
For you husband's coming home"
"Forgive our exaltation,
But we've been left alone"

"No doubt there are sound emotions,
That one day turned your head",
"Forget his deep devotions,
To us, your husband's dead!"

A life manipulating, bending of the truth,
Cajoling, stipulating, going through the roof,
Is over, and calm, descends upon the room,
A golden opportunity for talent new to bloom,

Body to Brain

"Mrs Jones! Our deepest sympathies,
For your husbands coming home"
"He has left us with instructions,
And he says he's on the phone."
"Be aware, we will ignore him,
I'm sure you'll understand,
We will survive regardless,
Despite the things he planned."

Precision, criticism,
Brutal put you downs,
Accomplished witticism,
Deriding hapless clowns,

Respite is now upon us!
The demon is put to rest,
His spirit exorcised,
For we all think that's best,

"Mrs Jones our deepest and most sincere sympathies,
For your husbands coming home,"
"We trust his wit will charm you,
Despite his face of stone!"

Stew Ross

I'm alright Jack

I'm alright Jack,
But thanks for your concern,
It's time to move along now,
There's nothing here to learn.

I'm alright Jack,
My bubble hasn't burst,
Remarkable, considering,
The way my life's been cursed,

Your sympathy's not welcome Jack,
So please leave me alone,
I don't require assistance,
No lifestyle chaperone,

I'm alright Jack,
My ducks are in a line,
My policy reached maturity,
My faculties are fine,

Your persistent interruptions,
Are playing on my mind,
It's time to bugger off now!
If you would be so kind,

Then I shall still be alright Jack,
Despite lack of your advice,
I don't need your encouragement,
Or help at any price,
I really can survive,
Astonishing as it seems.
Your thought that I relied on you,
Was only in your dreams.

So I'm alright Jack,
Really, I'm alright!
You appear to think I'm plagued,
Embroiled in sorry plight,

I shouldn't need to prove to you,
My life is running well,
You're surplus to requirements Jack,
Extraneous, can't you tell?

Disappearing Chances

The man in the pin stripped suit,
Tipped back his hat and spoke with authority:-
"A decision has been made, the position is filled,
As prescribed by the majority"

This comes as a shock,
As you realise your vote was not cast nor counted,
More over your chances were severely impaired,
As your campaign had never been mounted,

As your promotional aspirations fade,
The pathway obscured from view,
The power of assignations made,
Result in the downfall of you,

A mysterious game played only by fools,
With dismal consequences,
At the margin, not understanding the rules,
You stumbled at several fences,

You believed in rewards for efforts made,
That ends in disillusion,
Your contributions sadly under weighed,
Purged by corporate ablution.

Body to Brain

And Finally

He received two hours notice to clear his desk,
In reality, he only used one,
He kept two photographs and ditched all the rest,
Cleared his hard drive and then he was done!